HOW

COOK

BY
Susannah Bradley

ILLUSTRATED BY
Shelley Page

MACDONALD

First published 1979

Macdonald Educational Ltd
Holywell House
Worship Street
London EC2A 2EN

ISBN 0 356 063305 (paperback)
ISBN 0 356 063704 (hardback)

Printed by New Interlitho,
Milan, Italy

About this book

This book has been carefully planned to help you become an expert. Look for the special pages to find the information you need. **RECONGITION** pages, with a **bright blue flash** in the top right-hand corner, contain all the essential information to know and remember. **PROJECT** pages, with a **grey border,** suggest some interesting ideas for things to do and make. At the end of the book there is a useful **REFERENCE SECTION.**

The magic of cooking

It seems quite magical that all the different things on this page can be turned into a tasty meal of Spaghetti Bolognese, like the one opposite, doesn't it?

But if it *is* magic, then you too can be a magician – whether you're a boy or a girl, and whatever age you are.

Cooking is fun

Whether you want to cook for yourself, take over from your mother occasionally or entertain your friends, cookery is one of the most rewarding pastimes.

This book tells you the rules of safety and efficiency in the kitchen. Follow them carefully and you will find that cooking is much easier than you think. Above all, enjoy yourself!

Using this book

This is not a recipe book, although there are some recipes in it. Instead it deals with the methods and skills of cooking – so that when you have this book beside you, you'll feel more capable of tackling recipes in other books.

What to do

We tell you how to plan a meal, how to shop for the food for it, and how to make the most of your kitchen and the equipment in it.

The weights and measures in the book are all metric, but there's a conversion chart on page 59 if you come across recipes still in imperial measures.

◀You will soon learn how to combine all these ingredients and create a delicious meal.

▼Spaghetti Bolognese is splendid on a cold day! Don't forget the Parmesan cheese.

The kitchen

Find out which is the best chopping surface.

What's the first thing people do when they visit a strange place? They look around and begin to learn about their new surroundings. And that's the first thing that you should do in your kitchen. If you haven't been in there to cook before, you'll find a lot you don't know.

What to look for

Where are the pots and pans, gadgets and utensils kept? Where would you chop onions and dispose of rubbish? How many electric points are there; and where are the salt, pepper and other kinds of herbs, seasonings and spices stored?

When you know the answers to these questions, you are ready to start cooking. But first see if you can reach the working surfaces easily. If they are too high for you to work on comfortably, stand on a small stool or a wooden box.

Knowing your kitchen

It is very important to get used to your kitchen – so that you know at once where everything is kept. Then, if you need something in a hurry, you'll be able to find it immediately. Otherwise your sauces will go lumpy or your vegetables burn because you're busy searching for something at the last minute.

One of the best ways to get to know your kitchen is to help your mother in it. If you help her to wash up or watch her preparing a meal, you will gradually learn where things belong.

Always wash up your pans and utensils as you go along.

Kitchen equipment

Getting used to the things you use all the time in cookery is very important too. The cooker and the fridge, the kettle and some of the larger pans are familiar sights in every kitchen. Perhaps yours are slightly different from the ones we've shown here, but that won't matter – they all work in much the same way.

◀**Kettle.** Can also be electric. Always make sure the lid is on properly before you touch the handle.

▼**Pans.** The small milk pan is also useful for sauces. The larger pan can be used for vegetables. The pan below is a frying pan.

▶**Pressure cooker.** This steams food so that it cooks in a much shorter time. The manufacturer's instructions must be followed exactly.

◀**Cooker.** Your cooker may be gas, electric or solid fuel. This is a gas one.

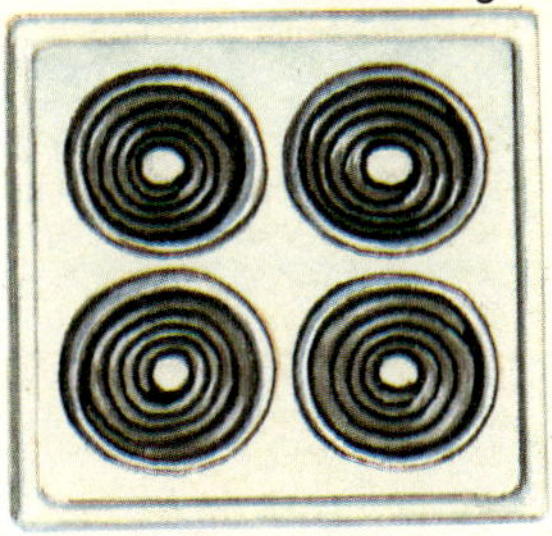

Most cookers have four **burners** (we've shown electric ones too) and a **grill** at eye-level or underneath the burners.

◀**Oven.** Usually found under the burners, but 'split level' cookers have a completely separate oven that is fixed to the wall.

A glass door allows you to check on food without causing draughts (and dropped sponges!). The warming drawer at the bottom keeps plates hot.

▼**Refrigerator.** This keeps food fresh and cool and has a freezer section for long-term storage of frozen food. Never put hot food or bananas in the fridge and always make sure that you have closed the door properly.

The tools you will need

Most cooks keep their equipment stored out of sight in cupboards and drawers – so you may not recognize some of the things shown here. They are the tools that every good cook needs, so you should learn how to use them all. Later you can start collecting your own.

▲**Mixing bowl.** Deep sides stop you scattering flour when preparing cakes or pastry.

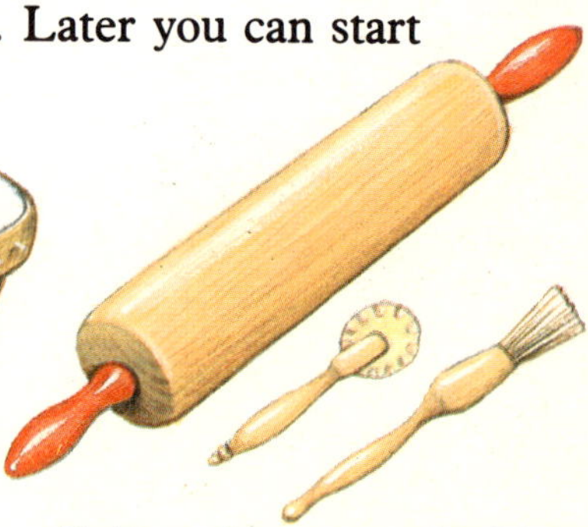

▲**Rolling pin; pastry wheel** for making a decorative edge and **pastry brush** for glazing a pie.

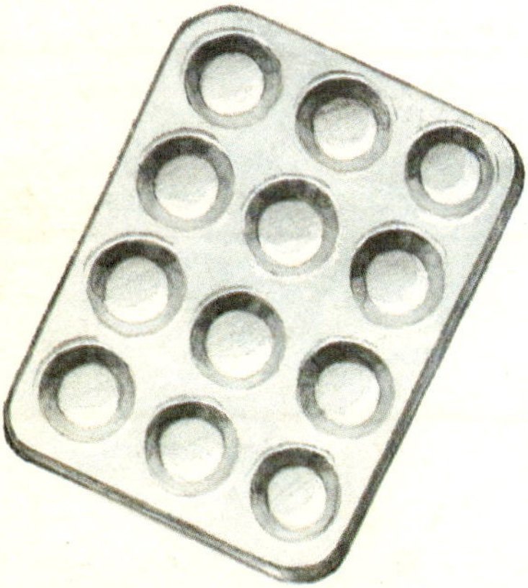

▲**Bun tin.** For baking tarts, buns and individual Yorkshire puddings.

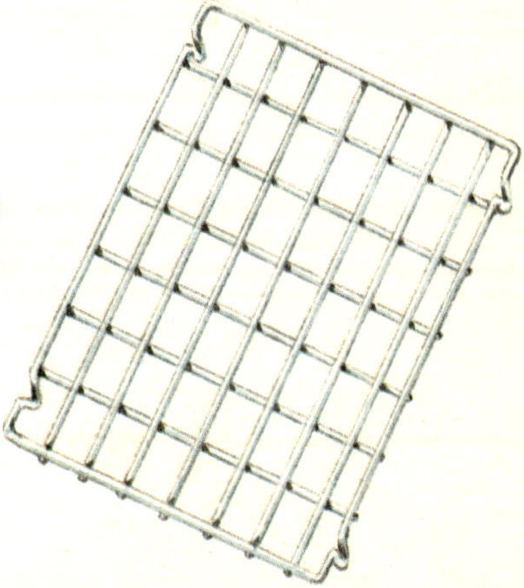

▲**Wire tray.** Cool hot cakes and pies on this: the air will circulate all round them.

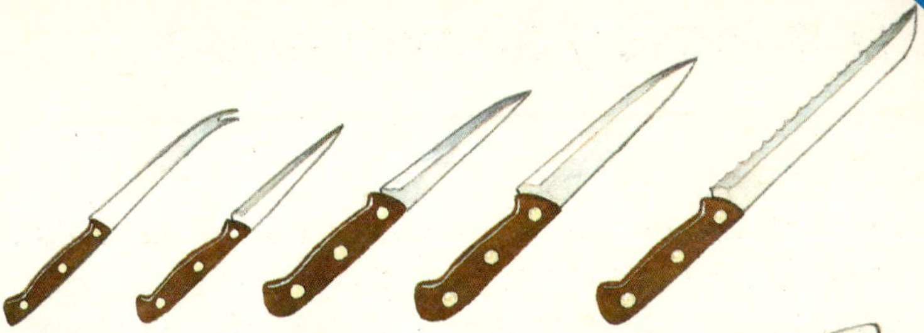

▲**Knives.** Take care, as they should be very sharp indeed. Otherwise they will bruise the food rather than cut it.

A serrated knife is useful for cutting tomatoes; use a broad bladed one for spreading. A vegetable peeler is good for taking a thin skin off potatoes.

▶**Tools:** for whisking, beating and stirring.

▼**Scales.** These are very important for weighing exact amounts. If you don't have the right quantities you may spoil what you are cooking.

▼**Colander and strainer.** These separate food from liquid. **Sieve** for refining soft food.

▼**Timer.** Set it to remind you that your meal is ready.

Nutrition

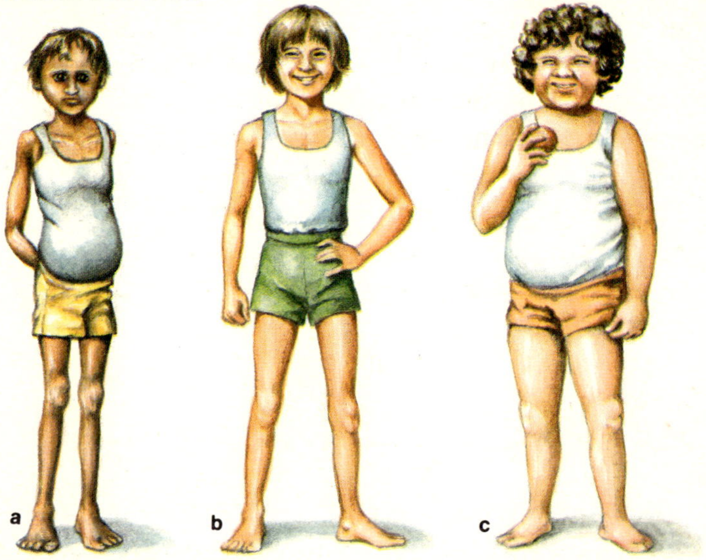

▲Lack of vital protein will make you very ill. This disease (a) is very common among children in tropical countries.

▲Too many carbohydrates are bad for us. A healthy child like this one (b) can easily put on too much weight (c).

To work properly our bodies need vitamins, minerals and balanced amounts of protein, fat and carbohydrates. We should make sure that our meals give us all these things.

Protein

Protein is the body-building food, vital when we are growing: found in meat, milk, fish, eggs, lentils and beans.

Fat

Fat keeps you warm and gives you energy. It is found in all fried foods, cheese, butter, milk, peanuts and sardines.

Carbohydrates
These supply energy quickly, and are found in all sweet and starchy foods. You need a certain amount of carbohydrate, or you will use up protein for energy and have no resources left to keep your body strong.

Too many carbohydrates in your diet will make you fat, so eat a reasonable amount only of: bread, cakes, sweets, sugar, rice, potatoes, jam, honey and pasta.

Minerals
Iron is necessary for good health. It is present in offal, spinach, watercress, eggs and chocolate.

Calcium is found in milk and cheese. It helps blood to clot and makes strong bones and teeth.

Vitamins
Vitamins A, C and D protect against infection and keep eyes, skin, teeth and bones healthy. They are found in fresh fruit and vegetables, eggs, fish and liver.

▼A sensible diet will give you shining hair and a clear skin, like this child's.

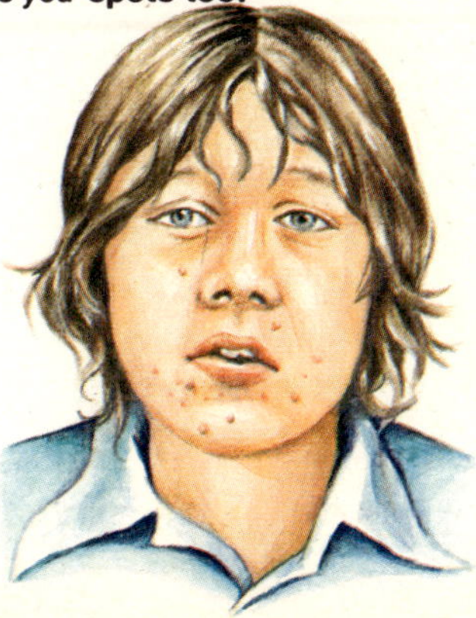

▼Too many sweets and not enough fresh fruit and salads will give *you* spots too!

Planning your meal

It is always better to plan your menu in advance, instead of dashing off to the shops and buying whatever you see there.

Try to use the foods that are in season as they will be cheaper and much easier to find (see page 61 for ideas).

Vary your menu

Your meal should suit the time of year. Serve thick soups and stews in the winter, salads and fruit puddings in the summer.

Remember what you have learned about nutrition and try to include lots of protein-rich foods like fish, meat, eggs, nuts and cheese. Avoid using too many stodgy foods such as bread, cake and pasta and remember that grease is bad for you too – so don't fry *everything*.

A balanced meal needs careful thought and preparation.

Going shopping

Go window shopping, and gradually you will become familiar with the different foods in season at different times of the year. Visit shops early, when they are quiet, so that you can ask the advice of your butcher, fishmonger or greengrocer if you need to.

Exotic foods
Many supermarkets stock a wide range of exotic foods and vegetables, and supply information on how to cook them, too. It is worth looking round a few days beforehand if you're giving a special dinner.

Fresh or frozen?
Always buy fresh food if you can, although frozen or tinned food can add variety, and are always better than tired vegetables or old meat and fish.

Tips and hints

Some tasks like separating an egg or chopping onions turn up again and again in cookery.

A good cook should know how to do these things in the safest and quickest way. Follow the hints on these two pages to learn how best to tackle these basic tasks.

Separating an egg

Some recipes, like meringues or choux pastry, ask for just the white (or the yolk) of an egg. Separate one from the other like this:

Use two bowls. Tap the egg sharply on the side of one of them and separate the two halves very carefully.

Let some of the white trickle into one bowl. Then rock the yolk backwards and forwards between the two halves of shell until all the white drops into the bowl. Then gently place the yolk in the other one.

let some white trickle out

Chopping an onion

Use a sharp knife, but be very careful.

Hold the onion firmly on the chopping board, and cut it in half from root to tip. Place one half on the board, with the cut side downwards. Now that you have one flat side, the onion is easier to handle. Make several straight cuts across the onion. Keep the pieces together, turn them round and chop them the other way. Now do the same with the other half.

parallel cuts

cross-cuts

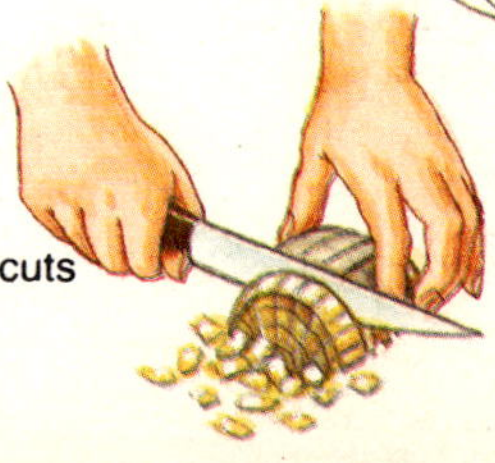

Chopping herbs or nuts

Place the herbs or nuts closely together on the chopping board. Use quite a large knife and make sure it is sharp.

Hold the knife handle firmly with your right hand, and take the tip of the blade in your left. Now move the knife blade up and down across the herbs, or nuts. Control the knife with your right hand, keeping the handle on the board. Move the blade with your left hand a few centimetres at a time across the ingredients.

Skinning tomatoes

When tomatoes are cooked, the skin peels off and tastes stringy and unpleasant. So it is much better to take the skins off first.

Boil some water in a saucepan. Then carefully drop the tomatoes into the boiling water, and leave them for one minute. Drain off the water, let the tomatoes cook, and the skins will peel off easily. Skin tomatoes for salads, too.

lower the tomato into boiling water

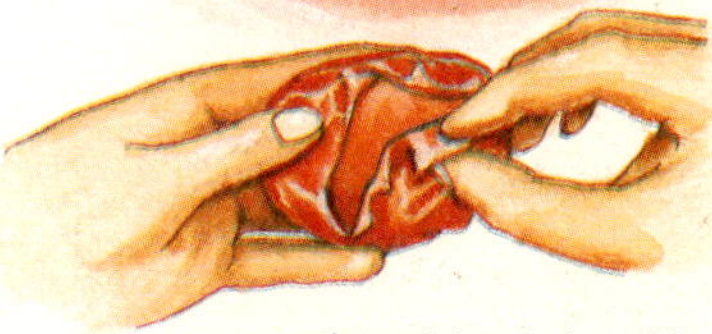

gently pull back the skin

Making breadcrumbs

Breadcrumbs can be used to coat fish or chicken.

Fresh ones are easily made in an electric liquidizer but you can also use up stale crusts. First dry out the crusts in a hot oven. Now put them in a paper or polythene bag and crush them with a rolling pin.

You can also use this method to make biscuit crumbs for cake bases. Store the crumbs in an airtight jar.

Using a timetable

Now that you have learnt some of the secrets of being a successful cook, why not invite some of your friends for a meal? But make sure that you avoid a situation like the one in the picture above, by planning each step very carefully.

Thinking ahead

Good cooks always work out a timetable to help them serve a perfect meal. So write down all the dishes and the time it takes to cook each one. It is a good idea to choose one dish that you can prepare the day before. If one of your dishes is to be served chilled, why not store it overnight in the fridge? Try not to choose more than one dish that needs a lot of preparation.

Some of the things that can happen if you don't use a cooking timetable!

Shopping list
Make out a shopping list of all the ingredients you need, and buy everything except fresh meat, fish or salad vegetables in advance.

The importance of timing
Decide what time you want to serve the meal, and work out the timetable of when to start cooking each dish. Work backwards from the serving time. Suppose two things are to be served together at six o'clock: one needs twenty minutes to cook and the other one hour. You should begin cooking the second item at five o'clock, and the first one at twenty to six. Remember that the oven needs at least ten to fifteen minutes to warm up beforehand.

Meat

Every cook should know how to recognize the various cuts of meat, what to look for when choosing meat of good quality, and the best ways to cook different cuts.

Look around carefully when you are in the butcher's shop. Try to remember the names and appearance of the different meats and joints, a few of them at a time.

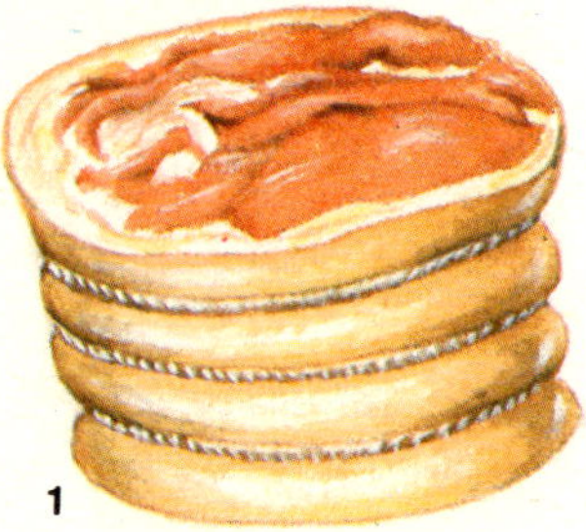

1

2

3

4

Beef

Good beef is bright red, with white, firm fat. Avoid meat with yellow, oily fat.

◀The joint of beef shown on the left **(1)** is a **sirloin,** which is very tender indeed. You can buy it like this, or cut into sirloin steaks.

Other expensive cuts are **fillet** and **rump.**

Slightly cheaper roasting joints are **topside, silverside** or **rib.**

◀Below the sirloin **(2)** you can see what a **steak** looks like, and how it is cut from the main piece.

◀Below that **(3)** is some **stewing steak,** cut up and ready to cook. Add some kidney to it to make a delicious pie or pudding. On its own stewing steak forms the basis of stews and goulashes. It is much tougher than the cuts for steak and joints, so it needs to be cooked at a low temperature for a long time.

◀Beef **mince (4)** is useful for many dishes, such as hamburgers, spaghetti bolognese and meatballs.

Pork

▶Pork is the uncured meat of the pig. It is a much paler meat than beef so it is easy to spot.

You must never serve this meat underdone; for if pork is not thoroughly cooked it can make you very ill.

A **leg of pork (1)** makes a good roast, especially if you rub salt into the skin to make it crisp.

Pork chops (2) are quick to cook and simple to serve.

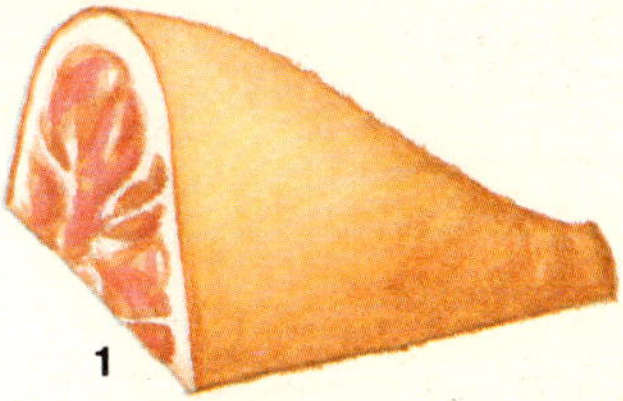

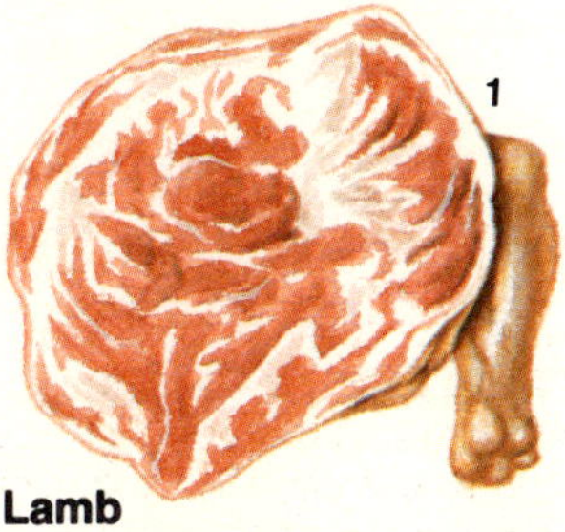

Lamb

You can roast **leg, shoulder (1)** or **loin** of lamb. Rub the leg with rosemary or a clove of garlic.

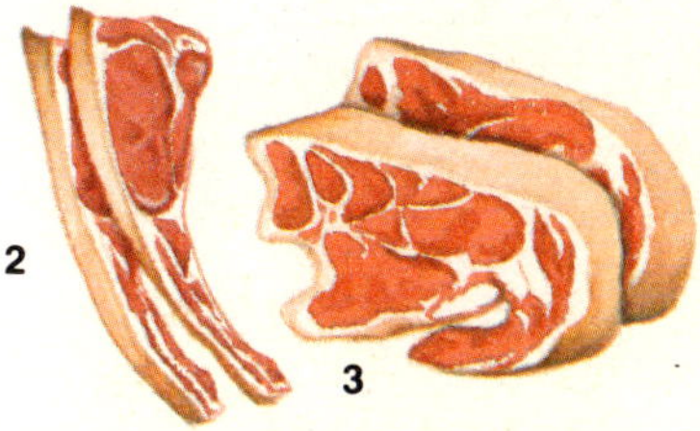

▲Allow two **loin chops (3)** per person: they are best grilled. **Chump chops (3),** cut from the leg, are more substantial.

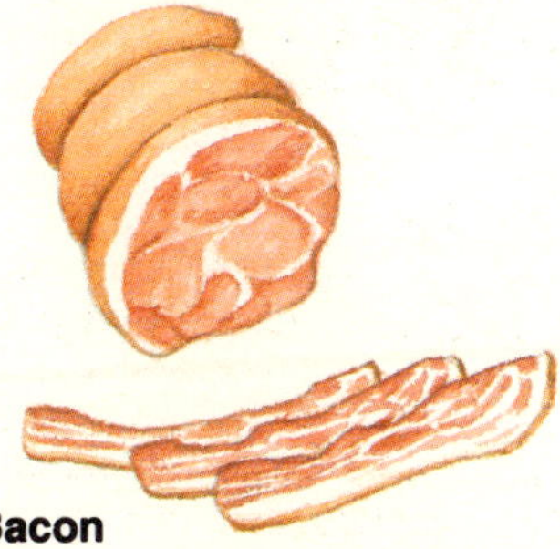

Bacon

▲Joints of **collar, gammon** or **hocks** may be boiled or baked.

Offal

▶**Liver, kidneys, hearts** and **brains** are all good for you; although the strong taste may be strange at first.

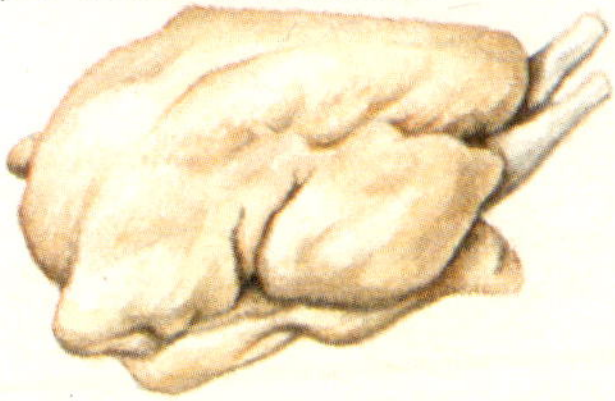

Chicken

▲Chicken may be roasted, used in casseroles, or fried. Lemon and tarragon, go well with it.

Roasts

Don't be frightened of using the oven. It's not difficult to use as long as you set the temperature correctly and keep an eye on the clock. Check your recipe book for the correct roasting times for each kind of meat.

Preparing the meat

Wash the meat and dry it thoroughly before cooking it. Always make sure a frozen chicken is properly defrosted and well cleaned out inside too.

Make cuts in the skin of pork and rub salt into the fat to make crunchy crackling. Lamb should have a spoonful of lard added to the roasting tin and some dried rosemary sprinkled on it to add flavour.

Always wear oven-gloves and an apron to protect your hands and clothes from hot fat and meat juices.

Stews

Dipping meat into flour before stewing will make it more tender.

When meat is cooked very slowly in liquid by simmering it gently on top of the stove, it is known as stewing. The same way of cooking meat in the oven is called braising.

This is a good way to cook tougher cuts of meat. They should be cut into bite-sized chunks, dipped and rolled in seasoned flour and browned in a little hot fat. Now add 'stock' – this is usually water, flavoured with a meat cube or drained from some previously cooked vegetables. The meat should then be left to cook slowly. Use this method to cook the famous recipe below.

Beef Stroganoff

Half kilo of chuck steak
Four tablespoons oil
One tablespoon flour
Salt and pepper
100g sliced mushrooms
Two sliced onions
Half litre stock
Two tablespoons tomato purée
Carton of yogurt

Cut meat into thin strips. Heat oil. Dip meat in flour, salt and pepper, and fry quickly. Fry onions until soft. Add mushrooms, stock and tomato purée. Simmer on low heat for 1½ hours, or until meat is tender. Stir in yogurt just before serving.

Frying and grilling

Frying and grilling are the quickest ways to cook chops, steaks, bacon, sausages, eggs and fish.

Keep the heat at a moderate level so that the food cooks evenly, and fat does not spit everywhere. Even so, you must take constant care. Grilled food is better for you than fried, as the fat runs out into the grill pan underneath it. Always make sure the food is dry before frying, or it will not brown properly.

Grilled food cooks quickly—so take care it doesn't burn!

Mixed grill

One loin chop
One kidney
One sausage
One rasher of bacon
One tomato
Mushrooms

These quantities are for one person. Cut the kidney in two, remove the white core and skin. Wash and dry the kidney and chop. Heat the grill. Put in the chop and sausage. Add the kidney five minutes later.

Cut off the bacon rind and put in the rasher. Turn everything as it cooks. When the chop is nearly ready, add the tomato, halved, and the mushrooms. Dot them with a little butter. Serve with a fresh green salad.

How to make hamburgers

►For two people use two onions, a quarter kilo of rump steak, minced, and a tablespoon of oil. Chop one onion finely; slice the other into rings.

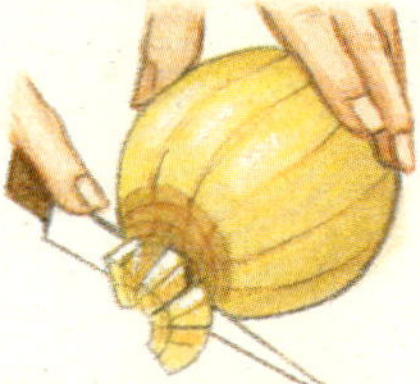

◄Heat the oil in a frying pan and cook the onions gently until transparent.

►Remove the cooked onion from the pan, and mix with the meat. Now add seasoning.

◄Divide the mixture in two and form each half into a flat round cake.

►Fry the meat cakes and onion rings over moderate heat. Add more oil if necessary.

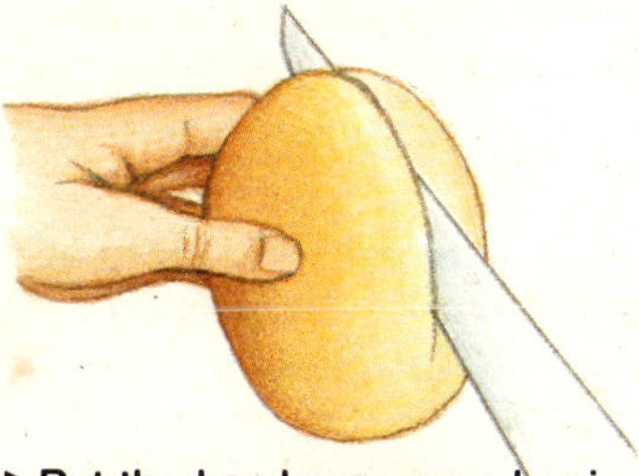

◄Slit two soft rolls or buns in half and toast lightly on the cut sides.

►Put the hamburgers and onion rings on the rolls and serve immediately.

Fish and seafood

Only buy fish which looks and smells fresh. The flesh should feel firm, the skin should still be gleaming and the eyes bright, not dull and flat.

A fishmonger will always clean and fillet whole fish for you – so don't be afraid to ask for his help.

How to cook fish

Fish can be grilled, baked, fried or poached. You should grill most types for about ten minutes but thin fillets will be ready in only two or three. Heat the grill first, then brush the fish lightly with butter or margarine and place them underneath it on a sheet of cooking foil.

Baking
Whole fish can also be buttered, wrapped in foil and baked in a moderate oven at 180°C (Gas 4). Steaks or fillets should be placed with a little liquid in a covered dish.

Poaching and frying
Poach fish by adding enough liquid (milk or water) to cover it completely. Bring it to simmering point in a covered pan and continue to cook for about ten minutes.

To shallow fry fish, use a small amount of fat only and coat the fish first (see below).

Egg and breadcrumb coating

One egg
One tablespoon flour
Breadcrumbs
A little water

Put flour in one bowl, egg beaten with water in another, and crumbs in a third.

Wash and dry the fish. Coat it in flour; dip it in egg and press into the crumbs.

Dipping fish in breadcrumbs.

Eggs

Eggs
Never run short of eggs. You can curry them, fry them, or hard-boil and take them on picnics. You don't like eggs? Why not try them converted into choux pastries, rich sponge cakes, soufflés, or meringues: or whip them into white sauces, custards and flans.

Eggs contain protein, iron and fat, so they are too good to miss. Don't keep your eggs for breakfast: they can be turned into splendid meals for any time of day.

▶Boiling eggs
Use a small saucepan. Do not use eggs straight from the fridge, as the shells will probably crack.

Bring some water to the boil in the pan. Then lower the eggs in gently. Boil for four minutes for a soft boiled egg, and nearer ten for hard yolks. Steep hard boiled eggs in cold water to avoid brown rings.

◀Scrambling eggs
Break an egg into a basin and whisk it up with a tablespoonful of milk and some seasoning. Now melt a knob of butter in a pan over a gentle heat.

Add the egg mixture to the melted butter and stir, on the heat, with a wooden spoon. Serve on buttered toast as soon as it is cooked. Add prawns or mushrooms for a supper dish.

▶Frying eggs

Heat a little lard or cooking oil in a frying pan but do not let it become too hot. Break the eggs into the pan and let them cook until the white is set.

Spoon a little of the hot fat over the yolk to cook it. Remove the eggs with a fish slice to avoid breaking the yolk.

◀Poaching eggs

If possible, use an egg poacher. This is a shallow pan with a tray on top of it. The egg containers fit into this, and are covered by a lid.

Boil some water in the pan, and lightly grease the egg containers. Drop in the eggs and put on the lid. Serve when the whites are set. This should be in about four minutes.

▶Omelettes

Use a heavy frying pan, and try to keep it for omelettes only. After use, rub it clean with kitchen paper.

Whisk two eggs in a basin. Add seasoning and a dessertspoon of water. Melt a knob of butter in the pan over a high heat. Drop the eggs in and fork them quickly from the sides.

This serves one person only.

Spanish omelette

One green pepper, chopped
One onion, chopped
Two tomatoes
One cooked potato

Fry the onion in a little butter. Add the pepper, cook it until tender. Dice the potato and tomatoes, and add them to the onion and pepper.

Make the omelette as above, in the omelette pan.

Add the filling when the eggs are creamy, but not quite set. Fork the mixture away from the sides and finish cooking. Serve flat on a warm plate. You can also add grated cheese, prawns or mushrooms.

Sauces

There are hundreds of sauces a good cook can use. Learn how to make just a few of them, and you will add variety and interest to your menus. Even if you only cook a few basic dishes, you will find that adding a sauce will transform each one into a different meal.

White and brown sauces

The most useful sauce is the white sauce, made from butter and flour cooked together with milk. It goes with vegetables, chicken, eggs or fish. You can add many things to it: herbs, onion, or cheese.

If the butter and flour are cooked slowly until brown, and then stock is added, it is called a brown sauce.

Cook the fat and flour together first.

Adding a cheese sauce.

A guide to sauce making

1. Always use the correct amounts of fat, flour and liquid.
2. To avoid lumps, cook the fat and flour well together before you add any liquid.
3. Never have the heat too high and stir continuously.
4. If you have to leave a cooked sauce standing, cover it until serving with a piece of dampened greaseproof paper.
5. Check the seasoning is right by tasting the sauce.
6. If there are any lumps, pass the finished sauce through a fine sieve.

Cauliflower cheese

One cauliflower
25 grams butter
25 grams flour
Salt and pepper
125 millilitres milk
75 grams grated cheese

Break the cauliflower into sprigs. Cook them for 15 minutes in boiling salted water. Save 125 millilitres of this water. Now make the basic white sauce. Melt butter over a low heat. Stir in the flour and cook gently. Add milk and water slowly, stirring until the sauce thickens. Then add the cheese. Pour the sauce over the cauliflower and serve immediately.

Mixing tastes

A quick look through the pages of a cookery book will give you an idea of which foods to serve together. Some of the combinations, like roast lamb and mint sauce, or gammon steaks and pineapple, will already be familiar.

▲Gammon garnished with pineapple has always been a popular combination.

▲Roast lamb with mint sauce or jelly is another favourite with most people.

Hot and cold

Other combinations may be less familiar. Try hot food with cold for an exciting change.

To make **hot chocolate sauce,** mix a tablespoon of cornflour to a paste with a drop of milk. Heat the rest of the milk with 50 grams of grated chocolate and 25 grams of sugar. Add the cornflour, and stir over a gentle heat for three minutes. Add a drop of vanilla essence, pour the hot sauce over ice cream and serve at once.

Try **Baked Alaska** too. Cover a block of ice cream with meringue, put it in a heat-proof dish and brown it in the oven for a few seconds.

Chinese food is well-known for its blend of different tastes and textures.

New ideas

Foreign dishes can teach us a lot about mixing tastes. One of the pleasantest things about eating a Chinese meal is choosing the food from the many bowls on the table, all containing something different.

Greek *mezze* is also tempting: salty black olives, cubes of tangy goat's-milk cheese, or yogurt blended with cucumber and garlic.

Try these combinations

Roast duck with orange sauce.
Chicken with lemon.
Roast turkey with cranberry sauce.
Lamb with apricots.
Melon with ginger.
Apple tart with cheese.
Pork with gooseberry sauce.
Roast beef with horseradish sauce.

Herbs and spices

Use herbs to bring out the flavour of a meal, and spices to add excitement. Fresh herbs are best, but dried ones are good too. Don't store them for too long as they lose their flavour. Below is a selection of some common herbs and spices.

▲**Mint.** As mint sauce (vinegar, mint and a little sugar) this is served with roast lamb. It also goes with potatoes and peas.

▲**Oregano.** You can use this in various soups and sauces. It goes particularly well with tomato dishes and salads.

▲**Parsley.** Add it to white sauce or use it as a garnish for soup, potatoes or fish. Use dried parsley very sparingly.

▲**Rosemary.** Use this to flavour shellfish and add it to meat dishes, especially rabbit.

▲**Sage.** This is most often used with onion in stuffing. But it can also be used in egg and cheese dishes for extra flavour.

▲**Thyme.** There are many different varieties of this herb, including a lemon one. Add to soups, stuffings and casseroles.

▲Tarragon. This suits chicken dishes very well; also used in soups, fish sauces and added to vinegar for salads.

▲Basil. This is ideal for all tomato dishes and sauces. Add it to pasta dishes too.

▲Chives. Chop these finely, and serve with cottage cheese in jacket potatoes or sandwiches, or use it in omelettes.

▲Garlic. Strong, so use sparingly! Rub a clove round a casserole dish: its fragrance will enhance the food cooked in it.

Spices

The easiest way to buy spices is in powdered form from supermarkets, or a good grocer.
Cinnamon. Is used in cakes and puddings, and sometimes in drinks, such as punch, too.
Cloves (shown). These are bought whole. Use them to spice a bacon joint, or to flavour baked apples.
Ginger (shown). Is used in cakes, gingerbread, parkin and puddings. It can also be sprinkled on melon.
Nutmeg (shown). This is most often used in custards. It may be bought as powder, or whole, for use with a grater.

Paprika. This sweet pepper suits mild foods such as shellfish, eggs and chicken.
Saffron. Comes in thin red strands and gives flavour to cakes, biscuits and rice.

Saffron is expensive, but you can flavour and colour rice equally well with **Turmeric.**

Vegetables

Vegetables add colour, variety and sometimes originality to a meal. It is impossible to show every vegetable; but here is a selection of the most useful.

▲**Green vegetables.** These are usually served as partners for roasts, grills and stews.

▼**Root vegetables.** These are often diced and added to soups and stews, but make splendid dishes on their own, too.

▲**Salad vegetables.** A crisp green salad is a pleasant accompaniment to grills, cold meats or fish.

▲**Less common vegetables.** These can add colour and interest to a plain dish.

▶**Pulses.** These are rich in protein. Lentils are often served with pork or ham, but they are also good cooked with tomatoes, peppers and onions.

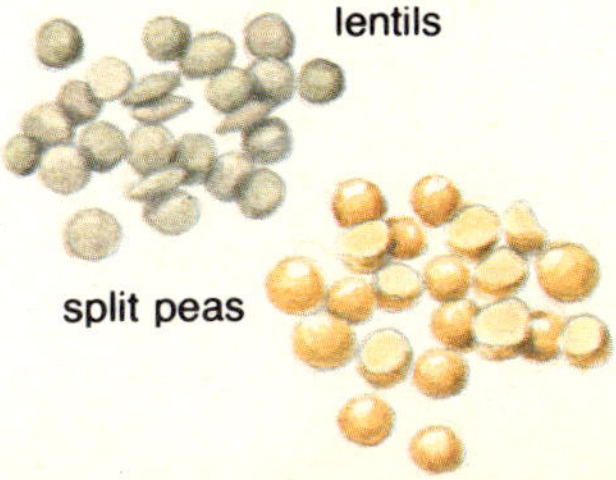

How to cook vegetables

Preparation

Peas and **broad beans** should be shelled before cooking. **Cabbages, cauliflowers, broccoli** and **Brussels sprouts** should have any wilted outer leaves discarded, and **spinach** stalks should also be thrown away. Remove the stringy rims on **runner beans** with a sharp knife. **Marrows** should be peeled, split in half and have the seeds removed, but **courgettes** can be cooked in their skins with their seeds left intact. All vegetables should be washed.

Cooking vegetables

Plunge green vegetables into boiling, salted water and cook for ten to fifteen minutes. Never overcook or delay serving them or they will lose their flavour.

Root vegetables

These can also be boiled, but as they often have strong flavours they are best suited to soups, stews and casseroles or to roasting with a joint.

Ratatouille

Two onions, four courgettes.
One red and one green pepper.
Two aubergines.
Olive oil for frying.
Seasoning. Large tin tomatoes.
Bay leaf.
Half teaspoon garlic salt.

Slice onions. Halve peppers, remove seeds and slice. Peel and slice aubergines. Slice courgettes thickly. Heat the oil, and fry onions gently. Add other ingredients, and season to taste. Simmer for one hour, or until vegetables are tender.

▼Ratatouille is a sunny Mediterranean dish and is delicious either hot or cold.

Potatoes

Potatoes can be peeled and chopped before cooking but they are just as delicious cooked whole in their jackets. Use old potatoes for this; large, evenly-shaped ones without blemishes are best.

Scrub them clean and prick the skins with a fork. Rub in some salt if you like the skins crisp. Bake in a hot oven, 200°C (Gas Mark 6) for an hour. Or, if you are already using the oven at a lower heat, put them in with whatever you are cooking and remove them when they are soft to the touch. Cut a cross in each one and serve with butter, chives or cheese.

In summer make a potato salad with new potatoes. Boil them for 15 minutes, drain, and slice them into a bowl. Pour some oil and vinegar dressing over them and let them cool. Serve with spring onions, mint and parsley.

Sprouting seeds and beans

Sprout seeds or beans at any time of year and you will always have unusual vegetables for soups, roasts or salads.

You will need a jam jar for sprouting seeds, and a larger jar for beans. Put a tablespoon of seeds or beans in to the jar, then cover it with a piece of muslin secured with an elastic band **(1)**. This helps when draining the seeds.

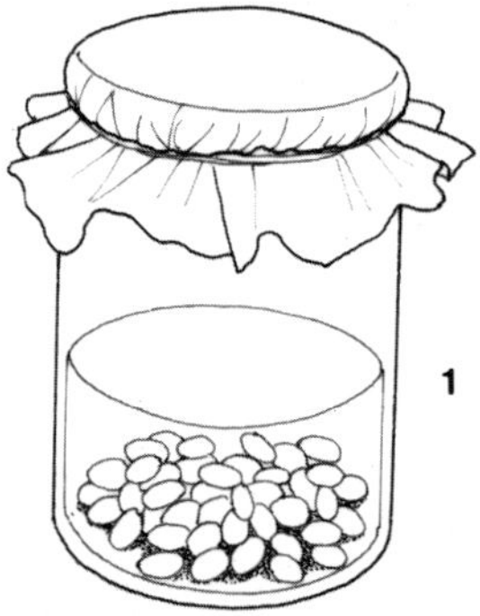

1

Fill the jar with lukewarm water, shake it thoroughly, then drain it. Do this twice more.

Leave the jar on its side to drain, preferably in a warm dark place **(2)**. Fenugreek seeds like a temperature between 13°C and 29°C.

Fill with water, shake and drain the jars twice a day until the sprouts are ready **(3)**.

They should take from three to six days to fill the jar.

2

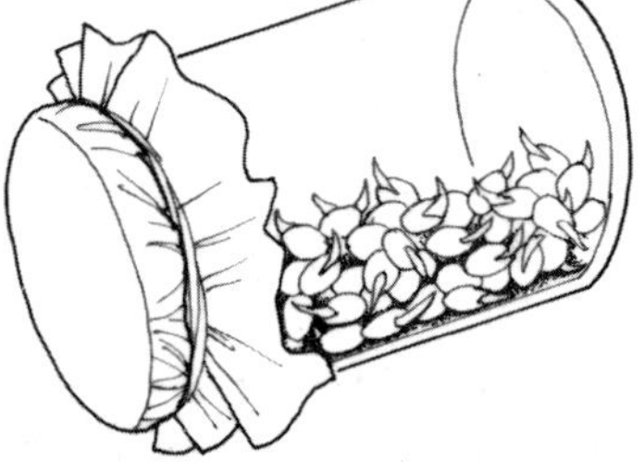

Chick peas, lentils, oats, rye, Aduki beans and fenugreek are all easy to sprout. Depending on which variety you choose, your seeds will yield from six to ten times their own weight in sprouts.

All sprouted seeds or beans are rich in minerals and vitamins. Make the most of their goodness by eating them raw in a salad. If rinsed well they will keep for several days in the fridge.

3

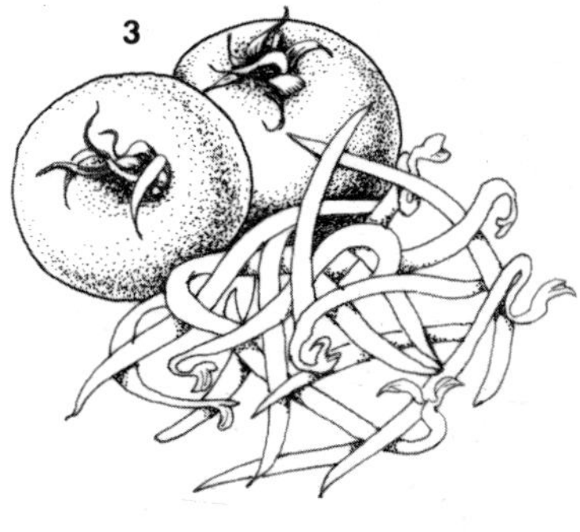

Pasta and rice

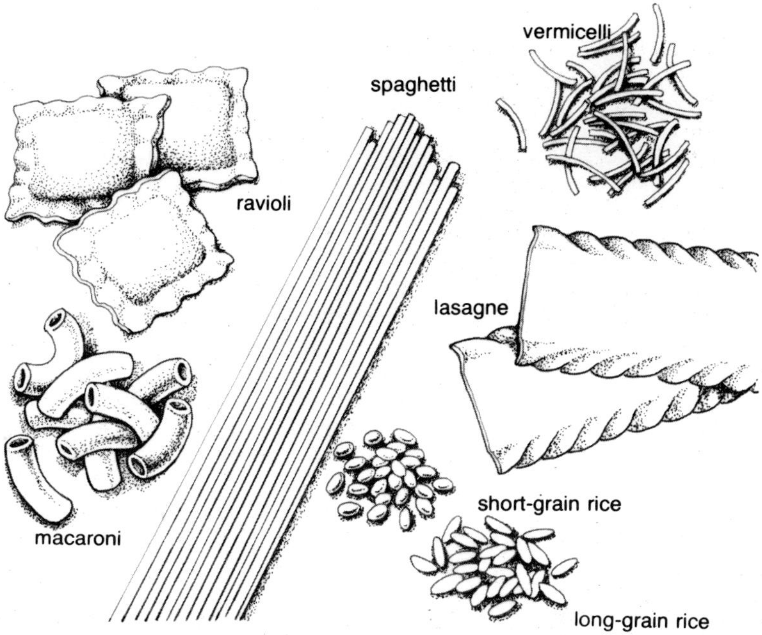

Pasta and rice often make a pleasant change from potatoes. But be careful! Both are very starchy foods so you should not eat them too often.

Rice
Long grain, or patna, rice can be served hot or cold, either with a main dish or as a risotto or kedgeree.

Pasta
All these types of pasta are variations of a basic dough made from semolina, wheat flour and water.

Cook both rice and pasta in plenty of boiling, salted water until they are just soft to the touch.

Salads

Salads are popular side dishes served with steaks, roast meats, fish and other main courses. They can also be a meal in themselves, if you add eggs, cold meats, or cheese. Make a **'salad niçoise'** by combining a green salad with tuna (or salmon), anchovies, cooked potatoes, French beans and hard-boiled eggs.

How to wash lettuce
Remove the outer, wilted leaves. Then, holding the lettuce by its stem, plunge it gently up and down in cold water to remove all traces of soil.

Dry it in a salad basket by swinging it round and round in the air, or let it drain on a clean cloth or piece of kitchen paper. Never serve lettuce that is limp and soggy.

Green salad

To make a green salad, wash a lettuce and separate the leaves. Halve, deseed and slice a green pepper and add cress or watercress. Mix together equal amounts of olive oil and vinegar, add salt and pepper and toss the salad in it.

Salad dressings

Mayonnaise: whisked egg yolk, wine vinegar and olive oil. The oil should be added drop by drop to prevent curdling and the yolks warmed slightly.

French dressing (or **vinaigrette**): a mixture of three parts oil to one part vinegar or lemon juice.

You can add variety to both dressings by adding different herbs, spices and seasonings. Add garlic or mint to French dressing, and chives to mayonnaise.

▲**Russian salad.** Peas, carrots, potato, turnip, French beans and beetroot.

▲**Coleslaw.** Shredded cabbage in a mayonnaise or vinaigrette dressing.

▲**Potato salad.** Cooked, cubed potatoes tossed in dressing when hot, and eaten cold.

▲**Rice salad.** Mix cold, cooked rice with peas, shredded red and green peppers, and onions.

Fruit

Make sure any fruit you buy is fresh and unblemished. Try to buy fresh, rather than canned or frozen fruit. Make the most of fruits when they are in season: citrus fruits such as tangerines and satsumas in the winter months; all the soft fruits of summer like blackcurrants, gooseberries, cherries, strawberries and raspberries; and young rhubarb in the spring.

Fruit makes a splendid snack on its own. It can also be turned into a fresh fruit salad, or stewed and served in sauces and pies. Why not try this recipe for a fruit pie?

Open Apple Tart. An attractive alternative to Apple Pie.

Fruit pie

150 grams shortcrust pastry
Half kilogram fruit
2 to 4 tablespoons water
2 to 4 tablespoons sugar

Prepare the fruit and place it in a pie dish with water. (Soft fruit will need less than apples or pears.) Add sugar to taste.

Heat the oven to 220°C (Gas 7). Cover the fruit with pastry. You may like to use a pie funnel in the centre. Cut a hole in the middle, trim surplus pastry, and use it to make leaves on top. Cook in centre of preheated oven for 20 minutes, and for further 25 minutes at 190°C.

How to make pastry

1. You will need 200 grams flour, 100 grams fat, cold water and salt. Sift flour and salt into a large bowl.

2. Chop fat into small pieces. Drop them in the flour, and rub the fat into the flour with your fingertips.

3. Use quick light movements and keep the mixture as cool as possible. Continue until the mixture looks like breadcrumbs.

4. Sprinkle drops from two or three tablespoons of water on to the mixture: stir it into a dough with a knife.

5. Place dough on floured board. Roll pin back and forth gently once or twice, then roll out firmly away from you.

6. Use a pastry wheel or a knife to trim off any extra pastry. Shape it into leaves for the centre of the pie.

Cakes

sponge with jam filling

fruit cake

There are cake recipes to tempt everyone from the most accomplished cook to the complete beginner. When you have made the basic Victoria sandwich, you may want to try a Genoese sponge (a whisked egg and sugar mixture which is very light), and fruit cakes, layer cakes, gateaux and birthday cakes.

Things to remember

Enjoy yourself experimenting, but do follow a few simple rules. Preheat the oven to the correct temperature. Weigh all ingredients accurately, and always grease and line your baking tins.

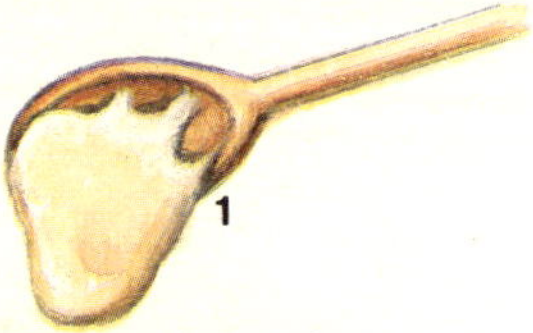

1

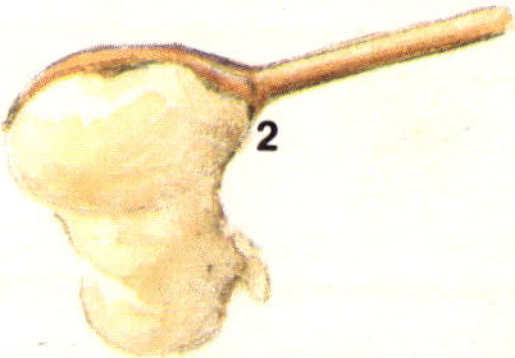

2

1. A mixture of **pouring consistency** should run easily from the bowl into the tin, or from a spoon into the bowl.
2. A mixture of **dropping consistency** is thicker: a spoonful will cling to the spoon for a few moments, before dropping back in the bowl.
3. A **firm dropping consistency** stays on the spoon and needs a flick of the wrist to make it drop.

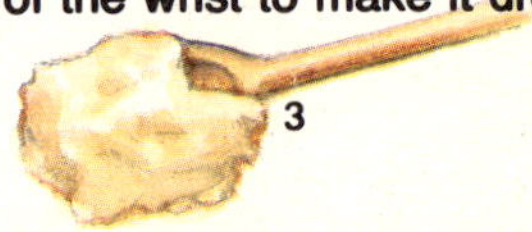

3

Rules for successful baking

1. If you are baking a fruit cake, prepare the nuts and fruit carefully. Rinse glacé cherries in warm water and pat them dry. After washing and drying the fruit, mix it with some of the flour measured out for the cake. This should stop it sinking.

2. When using the 'creaming' method, do cream the fat and sugar thoroughly, to break down the sugar. Beat in the eggs well, and fold in the flour quickly.

3. Test to see if the cake is ready by touching it with your fingertips. If no fingermarks appear, you can take it out. A warmed skewer pushed into the centre of a large cake should come out clean.

Victoria sandwich

100 grams butter or margarine
100 grams castor sugar
100 grams self-raising flour
Two eggs
Vanilla essence

Blend fat and sugar together for five minutes, until creamy **(1)**.

Whisk eggs and a drop of vanilla essence. Beat into the mixture a little at a time.

Sift the flour. Add a little to the mixture with the last few additions of the egg. Fold in the rest of the flour with a metal spoon very gently and carefully, so that you don't disturb the air bubbles in your mixture.

Grease two 16cm sandwich tins lightly, and dust with flour **(2)**. Put the mixture in the tins, and smooth down the surfaces.

Bake in the centre of the oven at 180°C (Gas 4) for 25 minutes. Let the tins cool, then upturn them on your hand. Cool the sponges on a wire tray **(3)**.

1

2

3

Decorating your cake

Cake decorating is fun. You can turn one simple cake into one of a dozen different ones!

Glacé icing

This can be used to cover any type of cake. Add two tablespoons of water to each 200 grams of icing sugar. Do this over a gentle heat and it will give the icing a glossy look. Add colouring, coffee essence, orange or lemon juice, or chocolate.

Butter icing

Use this as a filling or for piping. Beat 200 grams of butter with 240 grams of icing sugar to make a filling. Add three dessertspoons of milk if you want to pipe it. You can also add colouring or essences.

Using a piping bag

Your bag will be a plastic or nylon forcing bag, or a metal or plastic syringe, each with a selection of nozzles.

The nozzles will pipe shells, stars, rosettes, and writing. Unless your hand is very steady, write first on greaseproof paper, then prick the letters through it on to the cake. Pipe over the holes.

Always make sure there are no air bubbles in your bag or syringe before you begin.

Making sweets

Sweets
With a little patience and a steady hand, you can make some delicious sweets at home.

But take care if you are heating chocolate: it burns easily.

◀Coconut ice
300 grams icing sugar
150 grams desiccated coconut
4 tablespoons condensed milk
Cochineal, or other colouring

Mix icing sugar and condensed milk: stir in coconut. Divide this stiff mixture in two and add the colouring to one half.

Press one colour on top of the other in a greased tin. Leave until set, then cut into squares.

▶Peppermint creams
Half kilogram loaf sugar
35 grams glucose
6 tablespoons water
Peppermint essence

Dissolve sugar in water. Bring to the boil, stirring in glucose. When a spoonful forms a soft ball in cold water, take mixture from heat. When cool, add essence, roll out and shape with a bottle top.

▲Cutting out the sweets.

Sweets as presents
Save any pretty cardboard boxes you come across or line a shallow box with gaily coloured wrapping paper.

Wrap up your sweets in silver or coloured foil and arrange them in the boxes. Then tie up each box with a matching ribbon.

Sweets make very good Christmas presents or can be sold at your school fête or bazaar.

The importance of presentation

Always serve your food with 'care and flair'. Care means not slapping food onto the plates so that all the different foods are broken up and mixed together. Flair means using your imagination so that the food looks attractive enough to whet people's appetites.

Adding colour

A plate of sausages can often look rather boring. Liven it up with a sprig or two of parsley, and some pieces of tomato. Serve with Duchesse potatoes (finely mashed potatoes piped into whorls onto a baking tray and baked in a hot oven) and peas or grilled mushrooms.

Party food

This should look especially tempting, so always think ahead and imagine how the food is going to look on the plates.

Use cocktail sticks to make lots of brightly coloured tit-bits. Try combining a cube of cheese, a slice of salami wrapped around an olive, a gherkin and a grape. You could also combine a cube of fried bread with cheese, a cocktail sausage and a piece of fruit.

Experiment

Don't be afraid to experiment with different shapes and tastes. Try the combinations shown above, but use your own ideas too.

Small savoury biscuits make good bases for snacks or can be served with flavoured dips. Make sure the dips are not too stiff or the biscuits will crack in them. Arrange biscuits and cocktail sticks in patterns so that the plates look as attractive as possible.

Laying the table

A well-laid table is another important part of good presentation.

Use either a tablecloth or a place mat for each person. Put extra mats in the centre to protect the table from hot serving dishes.

The cutlery

This should be laid out as shown. If there is more than one course, the cutlery needed for the first course should go outside the main course cutlery. And don't forget the serving spoons!

As a final touch, arrange a few flowers in a small pot as a table decoration, or use candles.

Put a side plate on the left of each setting with a water glass above and to the right. The dessert fork should lie at the top, and spoon just above it.

Place a table napkin on the side plate, folded into a neat triangle.

Salt and pepper should be within easy reach of everybody.

How to fold a napkin

A beautifully folded napkin can make all the difference to your table.

Fold the napkin in half and then in half again, following the dotted lines in the diagram **(1)**.

1

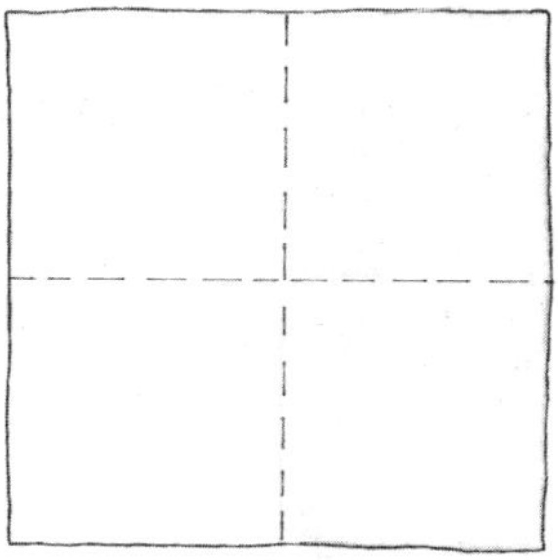

2

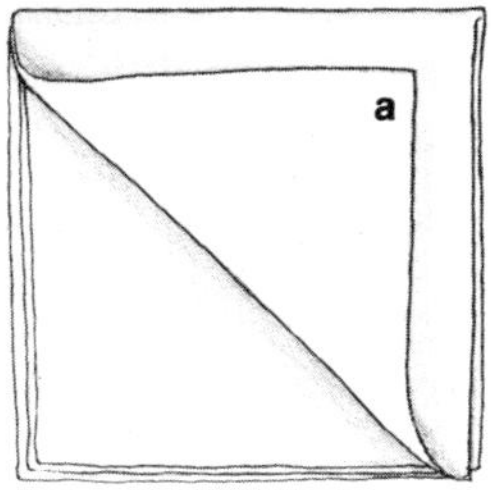

2. Lift up one of the corners and fold it back to within 5 cm of the opposite diagonal corner **(a)**.

3

3. Do exactly the same with the next layer.

4

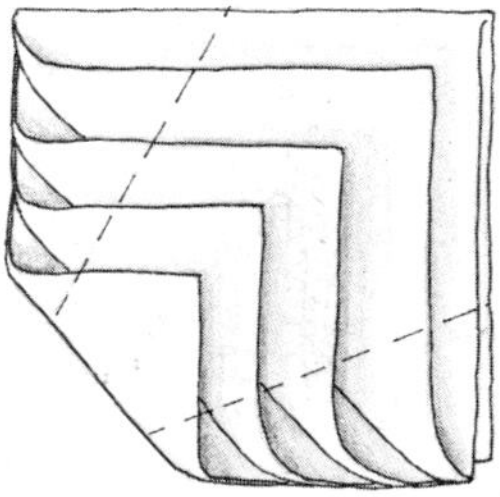

4. Fold back the last two layers, one at a time.

5

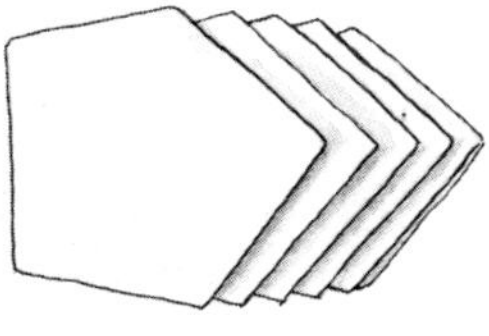

5. Now fold the sides under so that only the points show. You can even add a bow or some flowers just below the lowest point.

Clearing up

No one can help making a certain amount of mess while they are cooking, but there is usually a point where you can leave the cooking to look after itself, while you clear away some of the dirty dishes from your working tops.

Wash up as you go

Use all the pots, pans, bowls and utensils you need, but clear up after yourself as you go along. Soak used pots and pans in water as soon as you can: they will be easier to wash later on.

Have a bowl of hot soapy water in the sink, ready for used dishes. Wash them as soon as possible and stack them neatly on the draining board.

◀**Always check that you have remembered place mats for the hot dishes.**

◀The best cooks are clean and tidy people in the kitchen.

Before you serve the meal, give yourself enough time to make sure that the table is properly laid, and that plates and serving dishes are warm. It's silly to put hot food onto cold plates.

Clearing up

Afterwards, put any uneaten food you wish to keep in containers in the fridge. Stack all the dishes to be washed, and clear away table mats and tablecloth.

Wash cooking and carving knives separately, as soon as possible, removing any stains with steel wool.

Glasses, cutlery, pudding plates and side plates should be washed separately from any greasy dishes. Take care not to scratch enamelled pots or pans; really hot water should deal with the worst stains. Remember to wipe all the surfaces, and clean the sink afterwards.

Care and safety

Always use oven-gloves!

The kitchen is probably the most dangerous room in the whole house, so take great care when you work in it.

Tie back your hair so that you can see what you're doing. Keep yourself spotlessly clean and your utensils just as clean, otherwise you may contaminate the food. Make sure that all pan handles are out of reach of small children and wipe up spills immediately.

Golden rules of safety

1. *Never* touch an electrical plug, power point or appliance such as a cooker or toaster, with wet hands.
2. Keep all cloths and tea-towels away from gas jets, and never turn on the gas without having a light ready.
3. Always use oven-gloves to lift up hot pans and dishes.
4. Check that everything has been switched off when you have finished cooking.

Cover a burning pan with a wet cloth.

Fire!

If the worst happens and the grill or chip pan catches fire, what should you do?

Turn off the heat *immediately*. Then quickly soak a tea-towel in water and put it over the pan. You may need to use another one if the fire is really bad.

If this doesn't stop the fire, close the kitchen door, get everyone out of the house and call the Fire Brigade.

Every house should have a first aid box, and it is a good idea to have one handy in the kitchen where cuts or burns are likely to happen. You can easily put one together yourself.

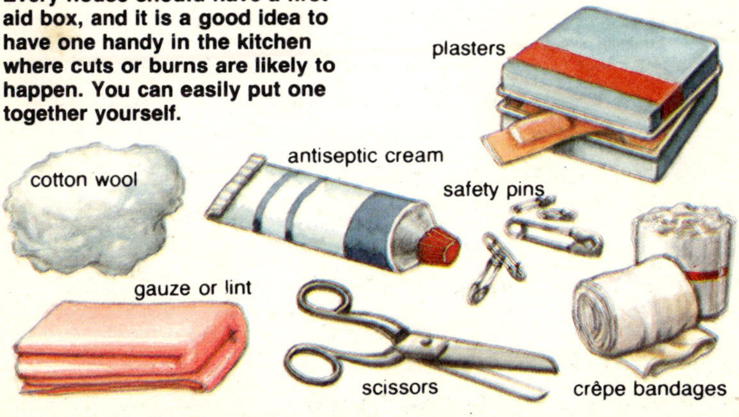

Reference section

Cooking terms

Baste: to spoon fat or liquid over food as it cooks.

Blanch: to plunge food into boiling water until partly or wholly cooked.

Blend: to mix ingredients together.

Bouquet garni: herbs (bay leaf, marjoram, parsley and thyme) tied up in a small muslin bag, and used to flavour soups, stews, and casseroles. Always remove it before serving.

Coat: to cover food, with flour, or batter, or crumbs.

Coating consistency: a sauce (or soup) just thick enough to leave a film of liquid on a spoon dipped into it.

Cream: to beat ingredients together until mixture resembles cream.

Dilute: to make something less strong, usually by adding water or other liquids.

Dust: to coat lightly with flour or sugar.

Flake: to break into small pieces; often applied to fish.

Fold: to mix carefully one ingredient into others, e.g. flour into a sponge mixture, or vegetables into a sauce. It is best done with a flat metal spoon.

Pare: to peel.

Pipe: to force a mixture (potatoes or icing) through a nozzle.

Poach: to cook food in a liquid which is boiling.

Purée: to turn solid foods (like tomatoes or raspberries) into a paste, using a sieve.

Roux: thickening agent of a sauce, made of flour and butter cooked together.

Rub in: to blend fat and flour, using your fingertips.

Season: to give flavour to food by adding salt, pepper and spices to it.

Simmer: to cook food slowly in liquid which is just below boiling point.

Weights and measures

The Imperial system of liquid measurement is still used occasionally in Britain: there are still pints of milk and beer, for example.

The old *avoirdupois* weights of pounds and ounces are fast disappearing however, although some recipes do still use them.

Below are two tables which will help you convert from one system to the other. If you remember one kilogram is 2.2 pounds, and one litre is about 1¾ pints, you won't go far wrong.

Ounces	Grams
1	30
2	55
4	110
6	170
8	225

You will see that these measurements are not exact. One ounce weighs 28.3 grams, but we have given the most reasonable equivalents.

Liquid measures

This table will let you convert from pints to litres, and millilitres (ml).

Pints	Litres
1	568ml, or ½ litre
¾	426ml, or ⅜ litre
½	284ml, or ¼ litre
¼	142ml, or ⅛ litre

One pint is exactly 568ml, but a generous ½ litre should normally be enough. Remember that when baking or making sauces, you should use exact measurements only. Don't be tempted to take short cuts.

Easy ways to measure

For day to day use, there are several handy measures it may help you to learn.

One teacup holds 4 ounces, or about 110 grams of flour.

If measuring liquid, a teacup holds 5 fluid ounces, or 150ml.

A generous tablespoon of flour holds about one ounce, or nearly 30 grams.

In liquid measure, a tablespoon holds 18ml. A dessertspoon holds about 12ml, and a teaspoon holds approximately 5ml.

Remember that the average British teacup is quite different from the breakfast cup, which holds about ½ pint or a generous ¼ litre.

A coffee cup holds 3 fluid ounces, or about 85 ml.

These measures apply only in Britain. American and Commonwealth cups, spoons and measures are quite different, so be careful when selecting recipes.

Useful charts

Cooking times for vegetables
Use this chart as a quick guide to vegetable cookery.

Vegetable	**Method**	**Time**
Artichoke (globe)	Boil	20 minutes
Aubergine, or egg plant	Peel: bake with butter and milk	30 minutes
Broad beans	Shell: boil	20 minutes
Brussels sprouts	Mark cross in base of each: boil	15 minutes
Cabbage	Shred: boil	10 minutes
Cauliflower	Break into sprigs: boil	15 minutes
Corn on the cob	Take off green leaves: boil	20 minutes
Leeks	Take off roots and leaves: boil	20 minutes
Mushrooms	Bake in covered casserole	30 minutes
Onions	Boil	60 minutes
Peas	Shell: boil	15 minutes
Spinach	Wash thoroughly; put in pan with salt: boil	15 minutes
Tomatoes	Halve, sprinkle with basil: grill	10 minutes
Turnips	Boil young turnips only: mash	25 minutes
Vegetable marrow	Peel: steam	30 minutes

Guide to oven temperatures in **Celsius** (C), **Fahrenheit** (F) and **Gas.**

Description	**C**	**F**	**Gas**
Very cool	110-130	225-250	¼-½
Cool	140-150	275-300	1-2
Moderate	180	350	4
Moderately hot	200	400	6
Hot	220	425	7
Very hot	240	475	9

Foods in season

Vegetables
The following vegetables are available all year: aubergine, beetroot, cabbage, carrots, onions, potatoes, turnips, mushrooms, lettuce, cucumbers, peppers, tomatoes.
Peas: May-October
Broad beans: April-July
Runner beans: June-September
Cauliflower: June-March
Broccoli: October-April
Marrow: August-October
Spinach: April-November

Fish and seafood
These are available all the year round: bream, cockles, haddock, halibut, lobsters, mullet, mussels, plaice, prawns, shrimps, sole, trout, turbot, whiting.
Cod: October-April
Herrings: May-November
Mackerel: March-July
Scallops: September-March
Skate: October-May
Sprats: November-March
Whitebait: February-September

Fruit
All year round: Apples, bananas, grapes, grapefruit, pears, pineapples, melons, oranges.
Apricots: May-August
Blackberries: July-September
Cherries: June-August
Gooseberries: July-September
Tangerines: November-February
Raspberries: May-August
Strawberries: May-July
Blackcurrants and Redcurrants: June-August

Protein foods

Remember how important the body-building foods are? The cheapest protein foods are milk and eggs but you may find people, especially small children, who don't like the taste of them unless they are 'hidden' in something else. The lists below should give you some ideas on how to make sure that everyone eats enough milk and eggs.

Foods containing milk
Cheese
Yogurt
Pancakes
Rice pudding
Blancmange
Yorkshire pudding
Junket

Foods containing eggs
Yorkshire pudding
Cakes
Pancakes
Fried food coated with egg and breadcrumbs
Meringues

Where to find out more

1. From other books.

All cookery books will have something new to teach you. Check the cookery section in your local library for new ideas and look out for the books listed below – they are particularly useful for the beginner.

The Young Homemaker, Book 1 by Angela Creese (Mills and Boon).

Full of good, simple recipes and housecraft.

Cooking Is Easy by Jane Todd (Beaver Books).

Packed with bright ideas for special occasion cookery.

The Zebra Cook Book by Maureen Williams (Evans).

Tells you exactly the order in which to do things, so you can follow the instructions word for word.

Cooking Around The World by Deborah Manley (Piccolo).

All the ingredients for these exotic dishes are easy to find and the instructions are well thought out and simple to follow.

Learnabout . . . Cooking by Lynne Peebles (Ladybird).

Useful for its many pictures of the food you are preparing.

2. From other cooks

Ask your mother, or anyone else you know who likes to cook, for ideas and advice on difficult dishes.

Try out everything before you decide that a certain type of cookery is not for you.

3. From newspapers and magazines.

Keep a cookery scrapbook, divided into sections marked Fish, Meat, Supper Dishes, Eggs and Cheese, Puddings, Vegetables, Cakes etc.

When you see an interesting recipe or useful tip, cut it out and stick it in your book. Try it out as soon as you can.

4. By experimenting.

Never be afraid to try things out for yourselves. Mix tastes and alternate ingredients.

This is the only way to be a really creative cook.

Index